WRITERS REPUBLIC

GOD'S POWER

FROM PRAYERS

JOSEPH MCGUIRE

WRITERS REPUBLIC L.L.C.
515 Summit Ave. Unit R1
Union City, NJ 07087, USA

Website: *www.writersrepublic.com*
Hotline: *1-877-656-6838*
Email: *info@writersrepublic.com*

Ordering Information:
Quantity sales. Special discounts are available on quantity purchases by corporations, associations, and others. For details, contact the publisher at the address above.

Library of Congress Control Number:	2021910393
ISBN-13:	978-1-63728-453-7	[Paperback Edition]
	978-1-63728-454-4	[Digital Edition]

Rev. date: 05/18/2021

I thank my Lord and Savior, Jesus Christ. The power of the Holy Spirit delivered me from alcohol and drug addiction, broken marriage, and bankruptcy. God restored victory in Jesus.

Introduction

Jayden and Dad's book is a physical proof of God's amazing power through prayers.

This is a daily prayer log for Jesus and the Holy Spirit to drive out all forces of Satan in Brooklyn Center and destroy them and to usher in a new era of very low crime rate, peace, joy, and love in our community and within our families and to start a great revival of Jesus in Brooklyn Center.

November 27, 2020
Friday
6:30 p.m.–8:00 p.m.

On my drive home in my Bonfe truck from my sister Rachel's house, where I helped move stuff from their house into the moving truck, I prayed a very powerful, passionate prayer that Jesus would bind and destroy all forces of evil, spirits, demons from Brooklyn Center and usher in lower crime rates. I also prayed that Jesus start a revival right here in Brooklyn Center.

The area crime notification went off as I neared the end of my prayer. There was a gunshot on Eighty-One, and I saw cop cars around the area. It is possible that satanic forces where lashing out as they were being driven out by the power of the Holy Spirit through my prayer. I can't be certain, just a thought.

I got home and was amazed at what I saw. The moon was so perfect looking, so clear in definition, and many stars were circled around my house. I've never seen the moon and the stars so close and clear or had them surrounding my home in that way.

November 28, 2020
Saturday

We kept praying daily for Jesus to remove Satan's forces from Brooklyn Center.

November 29, 2020
Sunday

We prayed the same prayer.

December 1, 2020
Tuesday
8:00 p.m.–10:00 p.m.

I am leaving my mom's house in Crystal with my son Jayden for a birthday get-together. Jayden and I prayed together very strongly that Jesus would remove Satan's armies from Brooklyn Center. Again, crime alerts went off in my area at that same time. We got home, and to our amazement, we saw the moon, so clear and defined and sitting full, and stars right one in our house. We agreed to start praying daily for God to lower the crimes in B. C. and remove all powers of Satan and start a Jesus revival there so we could track it. Once God answers our prayers, we can have physical proof of God's amazing power from prayer. We would then use it to witness to other people and bring them to Jesus. Again, we saw the turquoise color moving around on the camera. Very insane. Together we sang the song I wrote called "El Shaidi" while standing outside, looking at the clear full moon to honor Jesus. A beautiful moment.

December 1, 2020
Wednesday
5:30 p.m.

We again prayed in my room for Jesus to expel Satan's forces and for Jesus to bring peace and low crime in our city.

December 3, 2020
Thursday
5:14 p.m.

Jayden and I together prayed in my room that Jesus would bind all forces of Satan and all demonic activity and evil in Brooklyn Center, then destroy them and drive them out of the center. We prayed that Jesus would usher in lower crime rates, peace, and joy in all families. We also prayed that talk of Jesus would begin in this area and a great revival start in Brooklyn Center. We prayed to let this book be a powerful display of the supernatural power of God unleashing in our lives and making a difference in the community, that it will be a powerful testimony of God's power.

December 5, 2020
Saturday
3:00 p.m.–8:00 p.m.

Jayden and I prayed that Jesus and the Holy Spirit would destroy and drive out all forces of Satan in Brooklyn Center and usher in lower crime rates, peace, joy, and love in the all families and communities. We prayed that the talk of Jesus be present in B.C. and there would be a revival right here in our city.

December 6, 2020
Sunday
1:00 p.m.–7:00 p.m.

Jayden and I prayed again together that Jesus and the Holy Spirit would remove/destroy the forces of Satan and bring incredible low crime rates in our city and that other cities would have massive drop in crime rates. We prayed for laughter and peace and joy in all families. We also prayed that there would be a talk of Jesus in Brooklyn Center. We prayed that a great revival of Jesus would start in Brooklyn Center, 55249.

December 6, 2020
Sunday
6:51 p.m.

Jayden and I wrote a proclamation of Jesus, God the Father, and Holy Spirit to be recited daily.

Jesus, Holy Spirit, Almighty God of Abraham and Isaac, give ear to Jayden and Joseph and this family request.

Bind, remove, and destroy every demon and force of Satan and all evil spirits in Brooklyn Center and lower the crime to nearly zero, noticeable to all cities surrounding for Your Glory, Jesus, God Almighty.

Usher in peace, joy, love, and the talk of Jesus all around this city and start the great revival of Jesus and the Holy Spirit in Brooklyn Center. Amen!

December 7, 2020
Monday
8:44 a.m.

Jayden and I prayed in my room our daily prayer for Jesus to bind and destroy Satan, to lower crime rates, etc. During our daily prayer, we also spoke out loud proclamations of God Almighty.

December 8, 2020
Tuesday
12:40 p.m.–12:45 p.m.

In our living room, Jayden, my son, and I prayed our daily prayer for Jesus and the Holy Spirit to bind, remove, and destroy all demon forces in Brooklyn Center and to lower the crime rate so low that all surrounding cities would notice and talk about how low it is and how vastly it has changed. We prayed that they see God's power through our prayer and that God will answer prayers. We also spoke our proclamation to Jesus for Brooklyn Center.

My beautiful princess Kaylin is five years old and can't fully read yet, but she was present for the prayer and proclamation. She asked Daddy if I could read it slow so she could do it. How sweet! So as my princess sat on my lap on our couch in the living room, I said out loud our proclamation, two words at a time so she could recite it with me. We recited the entire proclamation. How precious a child so young on fire and interested in Jesus.

4:00 p.m.–6:00 p.m.

For the second time today, Jayden and I prayed for Jesus to bind the spiritual forces of Satan and all demons. We prayed that there would be low crime rate in Brooklyn Center and that it would be so low that the cities around would notice the massive drop in crime. We also prayed that there would be talk of Jesus all around and there would be a great revival in the city.

On the drive to my mom's house, Kerri, Kaylin, Jayden, and I prayed again this short prayer.

Before bedtime, in Kaylin's room, Daddy, Jayden, and Kaylin prayed again that God would remove Satan from Brooklyn Center. It was a very passionate prayer. Literally less than five minutes later, my ring camera neighborhood alerts went off with reports of gunshots going off a few miles away. Is this by random? Nearly every time we pray, some crime alerts goes off shortly after. It could be, but I don't believe so. Satan and the demon forces, when attacked with prayers, lash out. This was most likely that. Recent crime report maps in our area show how crime is being posted away from this area. This is the power of God from our prayer, waging war in the heavenly realms. Amen.

March 13, 2021
Saturday
8:30 p.m.

In our living room, my son, Jayden, and I prayed for God to drive all evil out of Brooklyn Center and to bring the revival of Jesus here.

As a father, I pray for each of my kids before bed. Our family prayed again for Brooklyn Center and thank the Lord for all His love.

March 18, 2021
Thursday

Jayden and I prayed again before bed. He wanted to sleep on the couch on nights when he has no school. We prayed again for our cities.

February 14, 2021
Sunday

We prayed together and thanked Jesus for driving out all spirits of Satan from this city and for lowering the crime rate. We also prayed that there would be a revival of Jesus in B.C.

March 3, 2021
Wednesday

Jayden and I spoke a powerful prayer together in my room. We both agreed we have missed too many days of prayer lately and need to continue and be persistent.

We prayed for Jesus to remove spirits of evil, and we thanked Jesus for lowering the crime rate and bringing about a great revival of Jesus in our city.

February 2, 2021
Tuesday
7:37 p.m.

Jayden and I said our proclamation out loud to Jesus. We cast out, in the Jesus name, all demonic spirits and asked our Lord to lower the crime rate and usher in a great revival of Jesus Christ!

February 9, 2021
Tuesday

In my room, we cast out all spirits of Satan in Brooklyn Center and called upon our Lord to bring the revival of Jesus Christ to the city and lower the crime rates in Jesus's name.

February 12, 2021
Friday

Another day of prayer for our city in Jesus's name.

Jayden and I spent a day biking around the city, planting gospel tracts and God's promise. Books all around and at little libraries. Our Hope is for kids in a tough society, to be able to read the good news of Jesus

We prayed consistently and passionately today, as we felt led.

January 21, 2021
Thursday
9:03 p.m.

In Kaylin's room, Kaylin, Jayden, and I prayed our nightly good-night prayer to bind and remove all spirits of evil in B-Center.

In Jayden's room shortly after, he and I spoke aloud our proclamation for B-Center and B-Park. We prayed for God to lower the crime rate and start the revival of Jesus. In the middle of our prayer, randomly and very loudly making noises, a police helicopter flew by. Not sure it has any meaning, but I made a note that we noticed it.

January 23, 2021
Saturday

Jayden and I prayed for Brooklyn Center, that Jesus would drive the crimes away from the area and that there would be a great revival of Jesus Christ.

January 18, 2021
Monday morning

Jayden and I prayed for our local cities while driving to Fleet Farm to get some new work pants for Dad's new job. It made us think of how every zip code in a COVID-19 world needs so much prayer. So we decided to pray.

Monday night

Jayden and I prayed for the second time today that God bring peace to our communities and usher in a revival of Jesus all around the world. We also spoke aloud our proclamation.

January 19, 2021
Tuesday
9:16 p.m.

Jayden and I spoke aloud our proclamation for God's victory in Brooklyn Center. We prayed together again in our basement Bible room.

January 24, 2021
Sunday

Jayden and I prayed for God to drive all spirits of evil out of Brooklyn Center in Jesus's name. We are committed daily, and trust that Jesus is at work.

January 26, 2021
Tuesday

Together Jayden and I prayed for God to bring revival and salvation to Brooklyn Center and for Him to drive all evil spirits of Satan out and drop the crime rate. Thank you, Jesus.

January 28, 2021
Thursday

We prayed again for God to lower the crime rate, drive out forces of Satan, and bring about a revival of Jesus in the city.

Jayden and I spoke aloud the proclamation to Jesus. Then we wrote a proclamation for Brooklyn Center and prayed together.

January 8, 2021
Friday

Jayden and I prayed again today for low crime rates and for the revival of Jesus to start. We have noticed a huge drop in crimes in our area. Praise Jesus.

January 9, 2021
Saturday

Prayed again, Jayden and I, for God to do His work in our city, removing and casting out the forces of Satan.

January 12, 2021
Tuesday

Staying persistent as we can, we again prayed today for peace in the B. C. area and the casting out of evil spirits.

In Jayden's room, we recited a powerful proclamation and a high-spirited prayer for B. C. and B. P.. We prayed to God to bring in the revival of Jesus, drive all spirits of Satan out of these cities, and lower the crime rate to nearly zero. Amen.

January 2, 2021
Saturday

Jayden and I prayed for Jesus to bind and destroy the spiritual evil forces in Brooklyn Center and bring in the talk of Jesus and usher in a great revival to the city.

January 3, 2021
Sunday

   Jayden and I prayed our daily prayer for Brooklyn Center. We included Brooklyn Park as well. We spoke aloud our proclamation to Jesus. After a great time with my family visiting, we praised the Lord in songs.

January 5, 2021
Tuesday

Driving with Jayden to Target in Crystal, we held hands and prayed for Brooklyn Center and Brooklyn Park. We thanked Jesus for all the victory in driving down the crime rate, bringing in a revival of Jesus all around this city.

In our living room, Jayden and I prayed for God to drive out all forces of evil in Brooklyn Center, to lower the crime rate, and bring the revival of Jesus in B. C.

December 29, 2020
Tuesday
4:04 p.m.

In my bedroom, Jayden and I took a pause from playing video games together. We spoke aloud our proclamation and again prayed for God's results to be shown in Brooklyn Center and Brooklyn Park.

December 30, 2020
Wednesday

Jayden and I continued in our daily prayer for removal of evil in Brooklyn Center.

January 1, 2021
Friday
8:45 p.m.

    Jayden and I prayed in my room to bind and destroy all forces of evil in B. C. Where two or three are gathered in prayer, God is there in the midst of them. We said aloud our proclamation.

    Also in our family devotions, we prayed together for the removal of all evil forces and recited what God was doing for our city.

I sent a friend of mine, my former cart attendant at Crystal Target and now a Brooklyn Center part-time police officer a picture of the crime map of my home In Brooklyn Center.

I said, "My home as you know is that red circle cross thing. Notice how crime is pushing away."

He said, "Ya, I work for BC, Medina, and St. Anthony. Been mega busy! He made mention of the crime appearing to be pushing away from my home area, was a great motivation to hear this from the outside!

I texted, "My son and I are writing a book. We have been since about November 28, 2020. Relay the message to your police chief. Please watch the power of God, Jesus, and the Holy Spirit. We have been praying daily that Jesus binds, removes, and destroys all spirits of evil and bring happiness, joy, and love to Brooklyn Center, and that there would be a crime rate so low in all cities around." So cheer us on as we aim to use God as the solution to inspire change.

December 15, 2020
Tuesday
5:00 p.m.–5:30 p.m.

Jayden, Kaylin and I prayed again for Brooklyn Center. We prayed that Jesus would lower the crime rate to nearly zero and that it would be noticeable to other cities around. We prayed that there would be a talk of Jesus all around and that He will bind and destroy all forces of evil. We also spoke our proclamation.

December 16, 2020
Wednesday
12:32 p.m.

    Jayden and Dad prayed for Jesus to bind remove and destroy all forces of evil in Brooklyn Center and usher in the great revival of Jesus all around, starting in Brooklyn Center. We also spoke our proclamation and sang our song to Jesus.

December, 16, 2020
Wednesday
8:00 p.m.

Jayden, Kaylin, Mommy, and Daddy had a short bedtime Bible reading and prayer. We prayed together for God's victory testimony for Brooklyn Center.

December 11, 2020
Friday
8:00 p.m.–9:30 p.m.

Jayden and I prayed again for God to remove all demons and forces of Satan from Brooklyn Center while we drove down Sixty-Third on our way to Target to buy a Nintendo Switch for my brother Josh's kids. We were singing the songs we wrote as well. It was beautiful. We also prayed for God to do His work in Plymouth MN, as we were at Target in this city. We asked for God to bring low crime rates, joy, laughter, and love to families.

December 13, 2020
Sunday
8:15 a.m.

In my bedroom, my family and I said our before bedtime prayer. Together we prayed for Jesus to destroy all evil in Brooklyn Center.

December 15, 2020
Tuesday
8:15 a.m.

In our room, Jayden and I did our daily prayer for Brooklyn Center, remaining steadfast in our prayer. I messaged my friend in the police department.

I said to Him, "Look at your crime rates in my area around 11/28. Looked to be pushing away. Give more patience to see more and more what the power of the Holy Spirit will do. My son and I will keep praying. Anything you need prayer for, bro?"

He responded at 8:22 p.m.: "Hey, man, that's good stuff. I'm good, to be honest. Thank you though!

I responded, "Praise the Lord, man. Ya let me know if there's anything. Ya have my support and the police."

December 17, 2020
Thursday
9:02 pm

In our living room, Jayden and Daddy prayed for Brooklyn Center. We recited a prayer to bind, remove, and destroy all evil spirits.

For the second time today, Jayden and I prayed for Jesus to bind the spiritual forces of Satan and all demons and to lower the crime rate in Brooklyn Center, so low that all cities around would notice the massive drop of crime happening. We prayed that there would be talk of Jesus all around and there would start a great revival in our city.

Shortly after, on the drive to my mom's house, Kerri, Kaylin, Jayden and I also prayed this again.

December 8, 2020
Tuesday
9:20 p.m.

Before bedtime, in Kaylin's room, Daddy, Jayden, and Kaylin prayed again that God would remove Satan from Brooklyn Center. It was a very passionate prayer. Literally less than five minutes later, my ring camera neighborhood alerts went off with reports of gunshots going off a few miles away. Is this by random? Nearly every time we pray, some crime alerts go off shortly after. It could be, but I don't believe so. Satan and the demon forces, when attacked with prayers, lash out. This was most likely that. Recent crime report maps in our area show how crime is being posted away from this area. This is the power of God from our prayer, waging war in the heavenly realms. Amen.

To destroy Satan and to lower crime, etc. is our daily prayer. Also, together we spoke out loud our proclamation to God Almighty.

December 8, 2020
Tuesday
12:10 p.m.–12:45 p.m.

In our living room Jayden, my son, and I prayed our daily prayer for Jesus and the Holy Spirit to bind, remove, and destroy all demon forces in Brooklyn Center and to lower the crime rate so low that all surrounding cities would notice and talk about how low it is and how vastly it has changed. We prayed that they see God's power through our prayer and that God will answer prayers. We also spoke our proclamation to Jesus for Brooklyn Center.

My beautiful princess Kaylin is five years old and can't fully read yet, but she was present for the prayer and proclamation. She asked Daddy if I could read it slow so she could do it. How sweet! So as my princess sat on my lap on our couch in the living room, I said out loud our proclamation, two words at a time so she could recite it with me. We recited the entire proclamation. How precious a child so young on fire and interested in Jesus.

Our family prayed that there would be massive drop-in crime rate in our city and it would be so low that other cities would notice it. We prayed for laughter and peace and joy in all families and there would be the talk of Jesus all around Brooklyn Center. We also prayed that a great revival of Jesus starts in Brooklyn Center, 55429

December 6, 2020
Sunday
6:51 p.m.

Jayden and I wrote a proclamation of Jesus, God the Father, and Holy Spirit to be recited daily.

Jesus, Holy Spirit, Almighty God of Abraham and Isaac, give ear to Jayden and Joseph and this family request.

Bind, remove, and destroy every demon and force of Satan and all evil spirits in Brooklyn Center and lower the crime to nearly zero, noticeable to all cities surrounding for Your Glory, Jesus, God Almighty.

Usher in peace, joy, love, and the talk of Jesus all around this city and start the great revival of Jesus and the Holy Spirit in Brooklyn Center. Amen!

December 12, 2020
Monday
8:44 a.m.

Jayden and I prayed in my room our daily prayer for Jesus's binding.

December 9, 2020
Wednesday
5:00 p.m.–7:00 p.m.

In my Bonfe truck with Jayden on the way to Marshalls in Crystal, Minnesota, we did our daily prayer for God to do His work.

6:00 p.m.–7:00 p.m.

Jayden and I on the way home from Marshalls in Crystal, we prayed again for God to destroy and remove Satan and his demon forces and usher in a great revival in our city and that there would be low incidence of crime.

8:00 p.m.

Jayden, Kaylin, and Daddy were having Bible time in the living room. Again, we prayed together for God to bind, remove, and destroy the evil forces. We kept getting phone calls disrupting prayer, people within the family arguing over silly things, finally we turned the phones off!

Satan attempted to interrupt our prayer, but we finished our prayer for lower crime incidence, for a Jesus revival to start in B.C., and for all cities to notice B.C.'s very low crime rate. Does anyone ever seem to notice these disruptions occurring in the middle of Bible time with family?

I am leaving my mom's house in Crystal with my son Jayden for a birthday get-together. Jayden and I prayed together very strongly that Jesus would remove Satan's armies from Brooklyn Center. Again, crime alerts went off in my area at that same time. We got home, and to our amazement, we saw the moon, so clear and defined and sitting full, and stars right one in our house. We agreed to start praying daily for God to lower the crimes in B. C. and remove all powers of Satan and start a Jesus revival there so we could track it. Once God answers our prayers, we can have physical proof of God's amazing power from prayer. We would then use it to witness to other people and bring them to Jesus. Again, we saw the turquoise color moving around on the camera. Very insane. Together we sang the song I wrote called "El Shaddai" while standing outside, looking at the clear full moon to honor Jesus. A beautiful moment.

December 2, 2020
Wednesday
5:30 p.m.

Again, we prayed in my room for Jesus to expel Satan and his forces, bring peace, lower the crime incidence in our city.

November 27, 2020
Friday
6:30 p.m.–8:00 p.m.

On my drive home in my Bonfe truck from my sister Rachel's house, where I helped move stuff from their house into the moving truck, I prayed a very powerful, passionate prayer that Jesus would bind and destroy all forces of evil, spirits, demons from Brooklyn Center and usher in lower crime rates. I also prayed that Jesus start a revival right here in Brooklyn Center.

The area crime notification went off as I neared the end of my prayer. There was a gunshot on Eighty-One, and I saw cop cars around the area. It is possible that satanic forces where lashing out as they were being driven out by the power of the Holy Spirit through my prayer.

I got home and was amazed at what I saw. The moon was so perfect looking, so clear in definition, and many stars were circled around my house. I've never seen the moon and the stars so close and clear or had them surrounding my home.

November 28, 2020
Saturday

We kept praying daily for Jesus to remove Satan's forces in Brooklyn Center.

November 29, 2020
Sunday

We prayed the same prayer.

December 3, 2020
Thursday
5:14 p.m.

Jayden and I together prayed in my room that Jesus would bind all forces of Satan and all demonic activity and evil in Brooklyn Center, then destroy them and drive them out of the center. We prayed that Jesus' usher in lower crime rates, peace, and joy in all families. We also prayed that talk of Jesus begin in this area and a great revival start in Brooklyn Center. We prayed to let this book be a powerful display of the supernatural power of God unleashing in our lives and making a difference in the community, that it will be a powerful testimony of God's power.

December 5, 2020
Saturday
3:00 p.m.–8:00 p.m.

Jayden and I prayed that Jesus and the Holy Spirit would destroy and drive out all forces of Satan in Brooklyn Center and usher in lower crime rates, peace, joy, and love in the families and communities. We prayed that the talk of Jesus be present in B.C. and start a revival right here in our city.

December 6, 2020
Sunday
1:00 p.m.–7:00 p.m.

Jayden and I prayed again together that Jesus and the Holy Spirit would remove/destroy forces of Satan and bring incredibly low crime rate in our city.

El Shaddai
By Joseph McGuire

Raging waves on the ocean floor
Defy the sound of the lion's roar
Lift your hands to the skies above
Shout with joy, my turtle dove
Singing praises to the Lord
Almighty God, my vengeful sword
My heart and soul will magnify
The news is good my El Shaddai

El Shaddai, He wages war for spiritual survival
Here I am, a servant of His great revival
O Lord, Illuminate my mind, so I may see
How to become the warrior in me

Yay though I walk through the valley
Of the shadow of death, I will fear no evil.

The Holy Spirit is with me and His
Angels prepare the way for me
Let God arise, and let His enemies be scattered

Hallelujah to the Lamb of God
Hallelujah to the Lamb of God

CPSIA information can be obtained
at www.ICGtesting.com
Printed in the USA
LVHW020834310821
696536LV00004B/165

9 781637 284537